Climate
CRISIS
The Science of **Global Warming**

by Don Nardo

Content Adviser:
Roberta Johnson, Ph.D.,
Director of Education and Outreach,
University Corporation for Atmospheric Research

Science Adviser:
Terrence E. Young Jr., M.Ed., M.L.S.,
Jefferson Parish (Louisiana) Public School System

Reading Adviser:
Rosemary G. Palmer, Ph.D., Department of Literacy,
College of Education, Boise State University

HEADLINE SCIENCE

Global Warming . . . Headline Science . . . Global War

Global Warming . . .

Compass Point Books • 151 Good Counsel Drive, P. O. Box 669 • Mankato, MN 56002-0669

 This book was manufactured with paper containing
at least 10 percent post-consumer waste.

Library of Congress Cataloging-in-Publication Data
Nardo, Don, 1947–
  Climate crisis : the science of global warming / by Don Nardo.
    p. cm. — (Headline Science)
  Includes index.
  ISBN 978-0-7565-3571-1 (library binding)
  ISBN 978-0-7565-3948-1 (paperback)
1. Global warming—Juvenile literature. 2. Climatic changes—Juvenile
literature. I. Title. II. Series.
  QC981.8.G56N367 2008
  363.738'74—dc22   2008007259

Editor: Jennifer VanVoorst
Designers: Ellen Schofield and Ashlee Suker
Page Production: Bobbie Nuytten
Photo Researcher: Svetlana Zhurkin
Cartographer: XNR Productions, Inc.
Illustrator: Eric Hoffmann

Art Director: LuAnn Ascheman-Adams
Creative Director: Keith Griffin
Editorial Director: Nick Healy
Managing Editor: Catherine Neitge

Photographs ©: Olivier Blondeau/iStockphoto, cover (bottom), 13; Len Green Photography/iStockphoto, cover
(inset, left), 15; Peter Van Wagner/iStockphoto, cover (inset, middle), 29; EcoPrint/Shutterstock, cover (inset, right),
10; AP Photo/Bela Szandelszky, 5; AP Photo/NASA, National Snow and Ice Data Center, University of Colorado,
Ted Scambos, 7; Weldon Schloneger/Shutterstock, 8; Tad Denson/Shutterstock, 11; Oliver Suckling/iStockphoto,
16; Jacek Chabraszewski/Shutterstock, 19; Jonathan Heger/Shutterstock, 21; Menahem Kahara/AFP/Getty Images,
23; AP Photo/Marco Ugarte, 24; Deshakalyan Chowdhury/AFP/Getty Images, 25; Guo Liliang/ChinaFotoPress/
Getty Images, 26; Gabriel Bouys/AFP/Getty Images, 27; Shaul Schwarz/Getty Images, 28; Ian Ilott/iStockphoto,
31; Anthony Ricci/Shutterstock, 34; Johannes Simon/Getty Images, 35; Toru Yamanaka/AFP/Getty Images, 37;
AP Photo/Sakchai Lalit, 39; Richard Schmidt-Zuper/iStockphoto, 41; Todd Arbini/iStockphoto, 42; mathieukor/
iStockphoto, 43.

Visit Compass Point Books on the Internet at *www.compasspointbooks.com*
or e-mail your request to *custserv@compasspointbooks.com*

122009
005644R

GLOBAL WARMING A THREAT TO EARTH

>>> ━━━━ ABC News
April 6, 2007

An international global warming conference ... approved a report Friday warning of dire threats to the Earth and to mankind ... unless the world adapts to climate change and halts its progress. ... [U]p to 30 percent of the Earth's species face an increased risk of vanishing if global temperatures rise 3.6 degrees Fahrenheit above the average in the 1980s and 1990s. Areas that now suffer a shortage of rain will become even more dry, adding to the risks of hunger and disease, it said. The world will face heightened threats of flooding, severe storms and the erosion of coastlines.

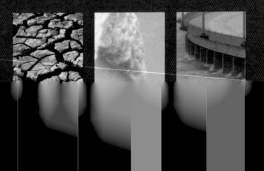

The planet is warming up. The world's living things—plants, animals, and humans—all feel the effects of this global warming. The term *global warming* refers to increases in the temperature of Earth's atmosphere. Such increases also cause water in the oceans and lakes to grow warmer.

A WARMING PLANET

Both scientists and ordinary people have noticed a number of signs of global warming over the past several years. For example, scientists found that of the hottest 21 years ever recorded, 20 of them occurred in the past 25 years. A recent year, 2005, was the hottest of all. All-time records were broken as temperatures soared and remained above 100 degrees Fahrenheit (38 degrees Celsius) across the United States and other parts

of the world for an extended period. Scientists also found that the overall temperature of Earth's atmosphere—the blanket of gases that surrounds the planet—rose at least half a degree between 1982 and 2007. That does not sound like very much. But even a small difference in temperature can produce major changes in climate. A good deal of evidence also suggests that the rate of atmospheric warming seems to be steadily speeding up.

A swimming pool in Budapest, Hungary, offered refuge from the heat when temperatures soared to more than 104 degrees Fahrenheit (40 degrees Celsius) in July 2007.

KEEPING CURRENT

News changes every minute, and readers need access to the latest information to keep current. Here are a few key search terms to help you locate up-to-the-minute global warming headlines.

alternative energy sources

climate change

global warming

Kyoto Protocol

National Center for Atmospheric Research

National Oceanic and Atmospheric Administration

Regional Greenhouse Gas Initiative (RGGI)

U.S. Intergovernmental Panel on Climate Change

MELTING ICE

Another sign of global warming is the retreat of glaciers all over the globe. Glaciers are enormous masses of ice that formed over thousands of years. When expanding, they move very slowly across the land. Hundreds of the world's glaciers have been rapidly shrinking in recent years. One is Grinnell Glacier in Glacier National Park in northern Montana. In the past century and a half, it has retreated a full two-thirds of a mile (1 kilometer) and is almost gone. Some other U.S. glaciers located in the Cascades Range in Washington and Oregon have lost 20 percent to 40 percent of their volume since 1984. The once-gigantic glacier atop Mount Kilimanjaro in the African nation of Tanzania lost 82 percent of its volume between 1912 and 2000. Experts expect the last of it to disappear by 2020.

Glaciers are not the only kind of large-scale ice that has been melting. The huge sheets of pack ice that formed over thousands of years at the planet's poles are also at risk. In January 1995, a large section of the Larsen Ice Shelf in eastern Antarctica suddenly broke apart. Then early in 2002, in the short span of 35 days, an even bigger section of the Larsen formation collapsed and disappeared. It measured 150 miles (240 km) long and

NOW YOU KNOW

The planet's Arctic pack ice may be completely gone by the year 2030, according to a 2007 estimate by the National Snow and Ice Data Center in Boulder, Colorado.

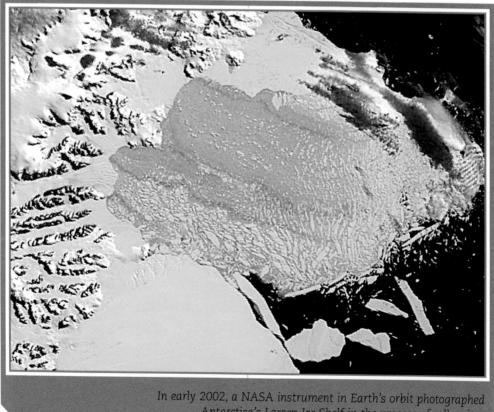

In early 2002, a NASA instrument in Earth's orbit photographed Antarctica's Larsen Ice Shelf in the process of collapsing.

Melting icebergs in the polar regions are a cause of concern for many environmental scientists.

30 miles (48 km) wide. In 2007, scientists noticed that large sections of the pack ice at the North Pole had thinned dramatically and had begun to disappear at an alarming rate.

EXTREME WEATHER

Still another sign of global warming is extreme weather. Experts define extreme weather as changes in temperature, rainfall, and so on that are more severe than normal. People are experiencing various aspects of extreme weather at increasing rates around the world.

Extremes in temperature are a good example. Many people wrongly think that global warming will cause warmer temperatures everywhere and that this will lead to a sort of global summer. The reality is very different.

Earth is tilted on its axis. The warmth from sunlight and other sources is never evenly distributed to all the oceans and land masses. This means that an overall rise in atmospheric temperature produces widely different climatic conditions in different areas. Some regions are indeed getting hotter while others are getting colder and having harsher-than-normal winters. Still other areas are experiencing swings back and forth, from unusually hot summers to unusually cold winters. Many regions are experiencing more intense rainfall and snowfall. This is because a warmer atmosphere can contain more water vapor that can fall as rain, snow, or other forms of precipitation.

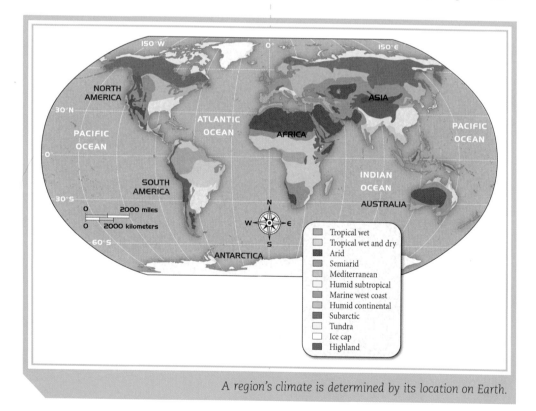

A region's climate is determined by its location on Earth.

Overall, global warming is leading to warmer temperatures and more intense precipitation.

The same sort of extremes can be seen in rainfall patterns. People in many parts of the world have noticed changes to centuries-old weather patterns. In Tanzania, for instance, people used to experience a predictable cycle of droughts. A local official explains how this has changed, making life for many Tanzanians more difficult:

In the past, we had a drought about every 10 years. Now we just don't know when they will come. They are more frequent, but then so are floods. The climate is far less predictable. We might have floods in May or droughts every three years. Upland areas, which were never affected by mosquitoes, now are. Water levels are decreasing every day. The rains come at the wrong time for farmers and it is leading to many problems.

In exteme drought conditions, parched soil cracks and separates.

Weather extremes are also caused by increases in the temperature of ocean water. This is best seen in hurricanes. These monster storms thrive on the warmth they draw from the ocean. Simply put, the warmer the water, the more energy a hurricane can pull from it. Some scientists think that they have observed an increase in the intensity of hurricanes that is related to the warmer water temperatures connected with global warming. The number of categories 4 and 5 hurricanes—the biggest and most destructive ones—rose by half between 1970 and the present. These large storms pose a greater threat to human and animal life. They also do extensive damage to cities and towns and erode and alter coastlines.

A variety of signs point to a rapid warming of our planet. The oceans are growing warmer, ice sheets are melting, and people around the world are experiencing extremes in weather. Evidence suggests that these changes will continue and worsen in the future.

Hurricane Katrina, which devastated the U.S. Gulf Coast in August 2005, came ashore as a category 3 hurricane.

HUMANS CAUSE GLOBAL WARMING, U.S. ADMITS

>>> BBC News
June 3, 2002

The U.S. Government has acknowledged for the first time that man-made pollution is largely to blame for global warming. ... In a 268-page report submitted to the United Nations, the U.S. Environmental Protection Agency (EPA) endorsed what many scientists have long argued, that human activities such as oil refining, power generation and car emissions are significant causes of global warming. ... "Greenhouse gases are accumulating in the Earth's atmosphere as a result of human activities, causing global mean surface air temperatures and subsurface ocean temperatures to rise," the report concluded.

Why have Earth's air and oceans been growing warmer in recent years? Scientists have proposed a number of theories to explain the changes. Most scientists think that the main causes stem from human activity. In particular, they say, people release various gases into the atmosphere. These gases are mainly responsible for the rises in temperature. Experts have come to use the term *climate change* to refer to global warming caused by humans. This is because such warming can also be caused by natural, nonhuman factors. Nevertheless, the terms *climate change* and *global warming* are often used interchangeably.

Because of the emissions cars produce, the rise in the number of automobiles in the world has contributed to the problem of global warming.

THE GREENHOUSE EFFECT

The idea that certain gases cause temperature changes in the atmosphere is not new. It has long been known that excess water vapor, for example, makes the air warm up. The same is true of several other gases, including carbon dioxide, methane, and ozone.

This happens because these gases have the ability to absorb and trap heat from sunlight. The effect is similar to what happens in a greenhouse. The sun's rays pass through the greenhouse's glass ceiling and wall panels and warm the air inside. However, the heat produced cannot

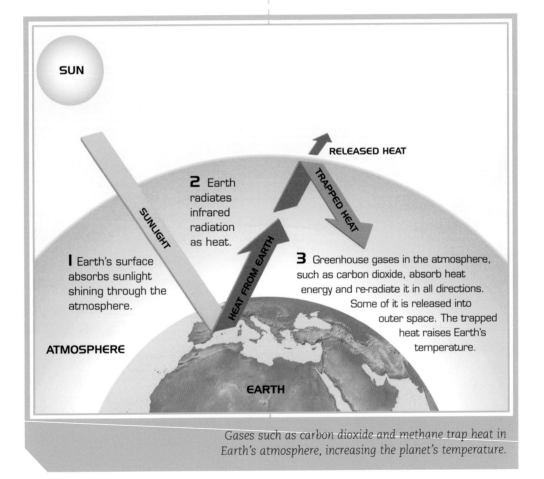

SUN

2 Earth radiates infrared radiation as heat.

SUNLIGHT

RELEASED HEAT

TRAPPED HEAT

HEAT FROM EARTH

I Earth's surface absorbs sunlight shining through the atmosphere.

3 Greenhouse gases in the atmosphere, such as carbon dioxide, absorb heat energy and re-radiate it in all directions. Some of it is released into outer space. The trapped heat raises Earth's temperature.

ATMOSPHERE

EARTH

Gases such as carbon dioxide and methane trap heat in Earth's atmosphere, increasing the planet's temperature.

escape because the glass traps it. After a while, the warm air that has collected makes it very hot inside the greenhouse.

In a similar manner, certain gases trap the sun's warmth. First, the sun's rays strike Earth's surface, warming it. Some of the heat then radiates upward, where the gases absorb it. Because of the similarities to a greenhouse, this is called the "greenhouse effect," and scientists have come to call these gases "greenhouse gases." The greenhouse gases—water vapor, carbon dioxide, methane, and ozone— have been warming the air for millions of years. This process long ago made the planet's environment warm and mild enough to support life.

PRODUCTION OF GREENHOUSE GASES

Some greenhouse gases, including water vapor and carbon dioxide, are a part of nature. The warming they produce naturally is normal and healthy for Earth and living things. What is not normal, a majority of scientists say, is when humans alter this system. They do this by releasing larger-than-normal amounts of greenhouse gases into the air. This causes more heat to be trapped in the atmosphere. The result is the unnaturally high temperatures associated with the growing climate crisis.

Some of the greenhouse gases that human activity spews into the air are

Human industry releases additional greenhouse gases into the atmosphere.

the same ones produced by nature. They include carbon dioxide, methane, and ozone. These substances are common byproducts of human industry and farming. A number of industrial processes create unwanted byproducts. Some of these byproducts, like soot, are solid. But other industrial wastes, such as carbon dioxide, are gaseous. These gases are also released when people or factories burn fossil fuels such as oil, gasoline, and coal. In addition, the greenhouse gas methane is generated by animal and human wastes. Large amounts of methane come from the huge herds of livestock that people raise around the world.

Human industries also produce greenhouse gases that nature makes only in small quantities or not at all.

Cows and other livestock raised in large farming operations produce the greenhouse gas methane through their waste.

Among these are nitrous oxide, sulfur hexaflouride, and various chlorofluorocarbons. (Chlorofluorocarbons, called CFCs for short, are used in refrigeration systems and some manufacturing processes.)

Of all the greenhouse gases that people produce, by far the most problematic is carbon dioxide, or CO_2. Not surprisingly, the amount of CO_2 in the atmosphere has increased since the beginning of the Industrial Revolution in the early 1800s. However, of that increase, half occurred between 1973 and 2006. This shows that the buildup

NOW YOU KNOW

Several billion years ago, carbon dioxide was much more plentiful in Earth's atmosphere, reaching levels as high as 80 percent. Today it makes up just 0.03 percent of the air, but it is responsible for about 60 percent of the additional atmospheric warming.

of CO_2 in the atmosphere is speeding up. If left unchecked, these levels will continue to rise, causing still more atmospheric heating.

THE EFFECTS OF FEEDBACK

Climate change is further complicated by other factors. For example, atmospheric warming caused by human activity can increase because of feedback processes. Feedback occurs when input and output within a given system form a loop and keep reinforcing each other.

One feedback process connected to global warming involves water vapor. When CO_2 and other greenhouse gases warm the air, more water evaporates from oceans and lakes. That pumps more water vapor into the atmosphere. Because water vapor is also a greenhouse gas, it proceeds to warm the air even more. In turn, the extra heat causes more evaporation, which raises the air temperature even higher, and so forth.

Ice and snow are key ingredients in another feedback process that affects

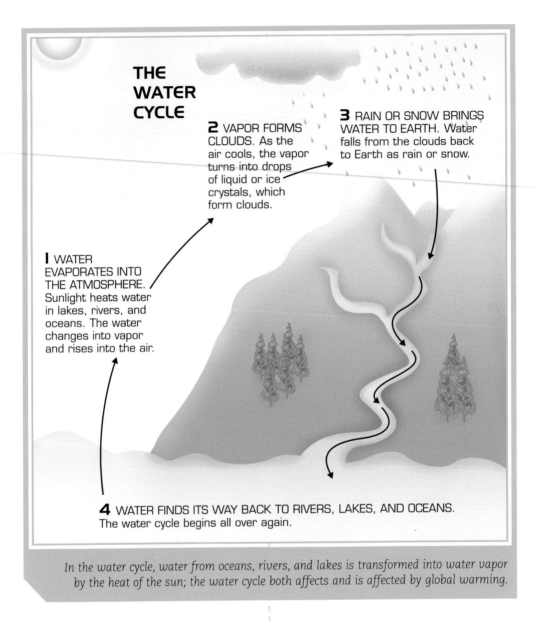

THE WATER CYCLE

2 VAPOR FORMS CLOUDS. As the air cools, the vapor turns into drops of liquid or ice crystals, which form clouds.

3 RAIN OR SNOW BRINGS WATER TO EARTH. Water falls from the clouds back to Earth as rain or snow.

I WATER EVAPORATES INTO THE ATMOSPHERE. Sunlight heats water in lakes, rivers, and oceans. The water changes into vapor and rises into the air.

4 WATER FINDS ITS WAY BACK TO RIVERS, LAKES, AND OCEANS. The water cycle begins all over again.

In the water cycle, water from oceans, rivers, and lakes is transformed into water vapor by the heat of the sun; the water cycle both affects and is affected by global warming.

global warming. Most of the sunlight that falls on ice and snow is reflected away from Earth's surface. This has a cooling effect on the air directly above, because heat is not held by the highly reflective surface. Obviously, if areas

Large areas of ice and snow reflect sunlight back into the atmosphere, preventing the light from warming the land.

covered by ice or snow expand, more cooling takes place. When combined with other factors, such a feedback loop can contribute to the beginning of an ice age.

The opposite happens, however, if the areas of ice and snow shrink. Warmer temperatures caused by global warming often melt ice and snow. More and more sunlight falls on darker soil or plants. These darker sur-faces absorb, rather than reflect, the heat. This causes both the land and air to warm up. As a result, even more ice and snow melts, further raising the temperature, and so on. Other similar feedback processes exist in nature. If enough of them acted together, they could greatly increase the effects of climate change.

NASA: DANGER POINT CLOSER THAN THOUGHT FROM WARMING ◼

>>> ━━━━━━━━▶ ABC News
May 29, 2007

Even "moderate additional" greenhouse emissions are likely to push Earth past "critical tipping points" with "dangerous consequences for the planet," according to research conducted by NASA and the Columbia University Earth Institute. With just 10 more years of "business as usual" emissions from the burning of coal, oil and gas, says the NASA/Columbia [study], "it becomes impractical" to avoid "disastrous effects." ... The forecasted effects include "increasingly rapid sea-level rise, increased frequency of droughts and floods, and increased stress on wildlife and plants due to rapidly shifting climate zones," according to the NASA announcement.

Scientists point out that global warming is already producing certain visible, measurable effects on the environment and human societies. Most experts think these trends will continue over time. If this does happen, there will almost surely be a number of negative results for Earth and humanity, as well as for plants and animals.

A lion drank from a shrinking pool of water in Kenya's Serengeti National Park.

RISING SEA LEVELS

One of these negative effects would be a rise in ocean levels (or an increase in the depth of the oceans). The new water from melting glaciers would certainly play a part. Scientists estimate that if the ice on Greenland and in the Antarctic melted, sea levels would rise by 23 feet (7 meters) globally.

Although climate models do not predict that this will happen, scientists are now seeing signs of instability in polar ice. Recently they have observed streams of water at the surface of the ice in Greenland during the summer. Some of these streams plunge down to the base of the ice, wetting the bottom of the glacier and helping it to move more quickly.

Scientists have also observed that the frequency of "ice quakes" on Greenland has increased five times over the past several years. This shows that ice on Greenland is cracking up. Some scientists are worried that this may be a sign of a further, possibly sudden rise in sea level that has not been included in their climate models.

But melting ice would not be the only factor causing sea levels to rise. As water warms up, it expands, taking up more space, so warmer waters would begin creeping shoreward. Also, floating ice sheets often hold back land-based ice sheets, keeping them from reaching the sea. As floating ice sheets break up, some land-based ice sheets will slide into the oceans. This will displace large amounts of water, causing further rises in sea levels.

Even small rises in ocean levels can have striking effects. For instance, a mere 1-foot (30-centimeter) rise in these levels would cause shorelines to move inland up to 100 feet (30.3 m) in some places. As oceans rise and storms become more intense, waves

NOW YOU KNOW

During the 20th century, sea levels along the U.S. East Coast rose 5 to 6 inches (13 to 15 cm) more than the global average.

caused by storms will ride farther inland. This will have an effect on communities that had previously been out of reach of the ocean. If global warming proceeds at its present rate, sea levels will rise 2 to 5 feet (60 cm to 1.5 m) in the next 50 to 100 years.

That means that thousands of beaches and millions of homes that now rest along them will be washed away a century from now. At the same time, portions of many coastal cities and towns will be flooded. Many nearby marshes, home to countless fish and

Waves crashed inland on the flooded shore of Lake Charles, Louisiana, after Hurricane Rita pounded the U.S. Gulf Coast in September 2005.

The continental coasts will not be the only areas destroyed by rising sea levels. Many low-lying islands around the world will simply disappear under the waves. Most of the Florida Keys will be gone, for example. Farmland located in and near the larger river deltas will be flooded. Most affected will be China and Bangladesh in Asia, Egypt in Africa, and Colombia in South America. Millions of people in these nations could become homeless. Meanwhile, a third of Florida might become part of the Atlantic Ocean. Much of the Netherlands in western Europe, a third of which is already below sea level, might be under water.

WATER SHORTAGES, DROUGHTS, AND WILDFIRES

Another result of rapidly melting glaciers will be a shortage of fresh water for drinking and irrigation. The problem may become especially big in India and other parts of southern Asia. For thousands of years, glaciers in the southern Himalayan Mountains have helped feed major rivers in the

Heavy rains in November 2007 submerged at least 80 percent of the Mexican state of Tabasco.

bird species, will be under water. Salt water will pollute all fresh water wells lying near the shores.

region. These rivers provide fresh water for more than 1 billion people—almost a sixth of the world's population. But these life-giving masses of ice are in danger of disappearing. Recent studies revealed that 466 of them lost 20 percent of their volume between 1962 and 2001. And their melting rate is speeding up.

Like many glaciers, numerous lakes will shrink and disappear as the world's air continues to warm up. This has already occurred in some places. The most famous example is Lake Chad in central Africa. Only a few decades ago, in the 1960s, it was the sixth largest lake in the world—about the size of Lake Erie in the United States. Today Lake Chad is only one-twentieth that size. Experts expect it to disappear completely sometime in the present century. Several factors have contributed to the lake's ongoing decline. Among them is overuse of water for irrigation by the 20 million people living near its shores. But perhaps the biggest factor has been lack of rainfall caused by a warming climate.

Villagers collected safe drinking water from a supply pipeline in Kolkata, India, on March 22, 2007, the World Water Day.

This warming of the air in many (though not all) regions of the globe has also triggered droughts. Large portions of the American West are experiencing record droughts. These are expected to worsen in the next few decades. The percentage of the world's lands affected by serious droughts has doubled since 1970, according to a recent study conducted by the National Center for Atmospheric Research in Boulder, Colorado. As a result, supplies of fresh water in various areas have been greatly reduced.

In addition to the loss of fresh water, large-scale droughts also dry out forests, prairies, and brush. This, in turn, increases the number, size, and destructiveness of wildfires. Because of dangerously dry conditions, a record number of forest fires occurred in the United States in 2007. As researcher Steven W. Running reports:

Large-scale droughts have dried up many sources of drinking water worldwide.

Since 1986, longer, warmer summers have resulted in a fourfold increase of major wildfires and a sixfold increase in the area of forest burned, compared to the period from 1970 to 1986. A similar increase in wildfire activity has been reported in Canada from 1920 to 1999.

Another unwanted result of the increased fire activity is rising levels of carbon emissions in the smoke from these fires. Some scientists worry that CO_2 and other gases in the smoke might prompt a feedback process. "If climate change is increasing [the number of] wildfires," Running says, "these new sources of carbon emissions will accelerate the buildup of greenhouse gases and could … [accelerate] global warming."

Wildfires in October and November 2007 devastated large areas in southern California.

INCREASES IN DISEASE AND EXTINCTIONS

Still another danger of climate change that scientists say is already happening is the spread of certain diseases. It has long been known that cold weather slows the spread of most germs. So it is not surprising that as some cooler areas warm up, they experience more disease. The World Health Organization tracks the global spread of various diseases. It says that climate change has brought higher temperatures and increased rainfall and humidity to a number of areas. These areas now have diseases they never had before in recorded history.

Illnesses that are spread by mosquitoes, such as malaria, encephalitis, and West Nile virus, are on the rise. Not long ago, Nairobi, the capital of the African nation of Kenya, had no mosquitoes. But rising temperatures and more rainfall have brought

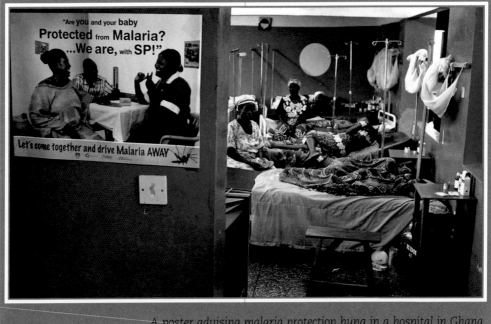

A poster advising malaria protection hung in a hospital in Ghana where many children were being treated for the disease.

mosquitoes, and with them increased rates of malaria. Similarly, before 1999, there was no West Nile virus in the United States. That year, however, unusually warm, wet weather allowed the virus to enter and thrive. Within only four years, it spread from coast to coast.

Humans are not the only living things affected by rapid changes in climate. Global warming has already sped up the rate of extinctions of many plant and animal species. Especially at risk are creatures that live in normally cold climates that are swiftly warming up. For instance, populations of arctic polar bears, emperor penguins, and cloud forest frogs are fast shrinking.

The case of the polar bears is a good example. Polar bears are good swimmers. However, as ice sheets grow thinner and break up, they must swim farther and farther in order to hunt and migrate. More than a quarter of them have died in the last few years, and they are increasingly endangered. Recent reports predict that 30 percent of polar bears will be lost by 2050. Also nearing extinction are the leopard seal, red-breasted goose, wattled crane, grey-headed albatross, bowhead whale, and many other species. Once these creatures are gone, they are gone forever.

HEADLINE
SCIENCE

Arctic animals such as the polar bear are at risk of extinction from habitat destruction caused by global warming.

A CHILLING POSSIBILITY

›› ▸ NASA
March 5, 2004

Global warming could plunge North America and Western Europe into a deep freeze, possibly within only a few decades. That's the ... scenario gaining credibility among many climate scientists. The thawing of sea ice covering the Arctic could disturb or even halt large currents in the Atlantic Ocean. ... Europe's average temperature would likely drop 5 to 10°C (9 to 18°F), and parts of eastern North America would be chilled somewhat less. Such a dip in temperature would be similar to global average temperatures toward the end of the last ice age. ... Some scientists believe this shift in ocean currents could come surprisingly soon—within as little as 20 years, according to Robert Gagosian, president and director of the Woods Hole Oceanographic Institution.

Scientists increasingly warn about the possible ill effects of global warming caused by human activity. These droughts, floods, wildfires, crop losses, diseases, and animal extinctions will occur in a world in which the atmosphere and oceans are, overall, much warmer.

However, there is another, very different future that global warming could create. It is a much colder one, in which large portions of the world become locked in a new ice age. It may not seem logical that increases in air and water temperatures could cause glaciers and ice sheets to expand

A possible and surprising outcome of global warming could be a new ice age, with decreased temperatures and increased snow and ice.

rather than melt. Yet evidence shows that just such a process has happened in the past. And under the right conditions, it could occur in the future.

A GIANT CONVEYER BELT

The ice ages were periods in which glaciers in northern, mountainous regions crept steadily southward. For thousands of years at a time, huge sheets of ice covered large portions of North America and Europe. As the glaciers moved, the ice crushed forests in its path and reshaped hills, valleys, and rivers. Living things, including primitive humans, either fled southward or learned to live in the ice, snow, and freezing temperatures.

The last major ice age ended about 10,000 years ago. But in the many centuries that followed, the Northern Hemisphere experienced several briefer cold snaps. Scientists call these "little ice ages." The two most recent examples took place from about 1150 to 1460 and from about 1560 to 1850. In the first of the two, massive glaciers covered Greenland. The cold conditions forced groups of Vikings, who had recently settled villages there, to pack up and leave. In the second of these minor ice ages, advancing glaciers in the Alps crushed numerous Swiss farms and villages. Canals in the Netherlands froze over. And in 1780, New York City's entire harbor froze.

The causes of these minor but destructive ice ages are somewhat unclear. But experts suspect that one major cause was a disturbance of normal water currents in the Atlantic Ocean. These currents make up what scientists call the Atlantic conveyer belt. Usually warm water in the ocean's upper layer moves northward, cooling little by little as it goes. When it arrives in the northern portion of the Atlantic, the cooled water sinks. This happens because cold water is denser than warm water. Next, having reached the ocean floor, the water begins traveling slowly but steadily southward. So there exists in the Atlantic a large-scale flow of warm and cold waters. The continual flow of warm surface water

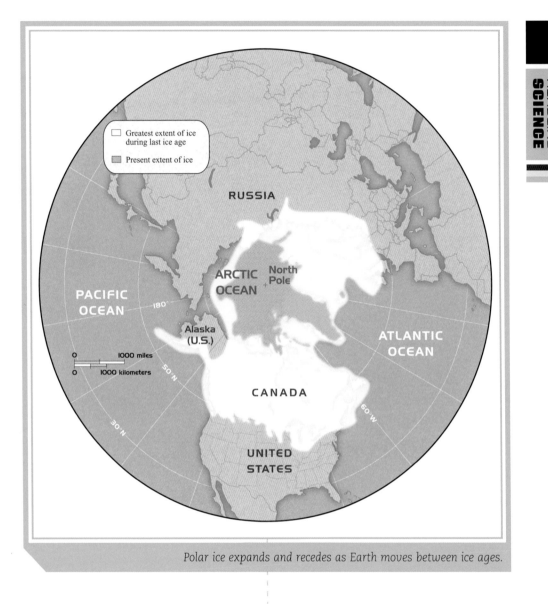

Polar ice expands and recedes as Earth moves between ice ages.

into the North Atlantic helps keep temperatures in the Northern Hemisphere moderate.

WARMTH TRIGGERS A COOLING TREND

Evidence suggests that now and then certain outside forces hinder this immense water circulation process. For example, a warming trend can cause some of the ice in Greenland and other northern regions to melt. This sends millions of gallons of fresh water flowing into the northern Atlantic. The problem is that fresh water is less dense than salt water.

The fresh water stays mostly on the surface and keeps the warmer water from the south from flowing in. The surface of the North Atlantic remains cold, setting in motion a cooling trend in the Northern Hemisphere. If the Atlantic conveyer belt is slowed down long enough, that trend can turn into

Because of global warming, glaciers on Greenland are slipping into the ocean twice as fast as they were just five years ago. They are losing as much as 36 cubic miles (150 cubic kilometers) per year.

a minor ice age.

Several experts worry that this may happen again in the near future. Among them are members of the Woods Hole Oceanographic Institution and the National Oceanic and Atmospheric Administration. Glaciers and ice sheets in the Arctic are already beginning to melt, they warn. And if the present global warming trend continues, increasing amounts of fresh water will be released. This water will pour into the North Atlantic. There, it might interfere with the Atlantic conveyer belt. In turn, this might trigger a cold snap in which the ice sheets rapidly return and expand. Canada, the northern United States, and most of Europe would experience much longer and colder winters than normal.

Scientists cannot say for sure whether this grim situation will take place.

But they would rather not find out the hard way—by watching it happen. They and other concerned individuals are actively promoting ways to slow or stop ongoing climate change.

In 2007, Munich, Germany, experienced an unusually cold, snowy winter after a decade of warmer weather.

E.U. RAISES BAR IN FIGHT AGAINST GLOBAL WARMING ▸

>>> ▶ *The Washington Post*
March 10, 2007

European Union leaders agreed Friday to take the 27-country bloc beyond the targets of the 1997 Kyoto Protocol on global warming, agreeing to legally binding reductions in greenhouse gas emissions and increasing the use of renewable energy. During a sometimes contentious two-day meeting in Brussels, the leaders agreed to cut the gas emissions by at least 20 percent from 1990 levels in the next 13 years. They set binding targets for renewable energy sources, such as wind, solar and hydro power, to supply 20 percent of the union's power needs and for biofuels to be used in 10 percent of the bloc's road vehicles by 2020.

The past two decades have witnessed two large-scale international efforts related to global warming. Both remain ongoing. One consists of numerous scientific studies dedicated to understanding global warming and predicting its effects. The other consists of attempts by various countries, states, and individuals to halt, or at least to slow, its progress. Some progress has been made in the fight against global warming. But scientists warn that a great deal more must be done to eliminate the threat it poses to Earth and humanity.

INTERNATIONAL AND REGIONAL EFFORTS

The United Nations (U.N.) sponsored the first international effort to address the problem of large-scale climate change. It became known as the Kyoto Protocol, because the meeting that produced it, held in December 1997,

Representatives from about 170 countries drafted the Kyoto Protocol in December 1997 at the United Nations Framework Convention on Climate Change.

took place in Kyoto, Japan. The main goal of the countries that met was to reduce emissions of greenhouse gases as much as possible.

These nations were divided into two groups: developed countries and developing countries. Under the agreement, developed countries were obliged to limit their greenhouse gas emissions by set amounts. Developing countries were not required to reduce their greenhouse gas emissions because doing so presented an economic hardship.

Most countries in the world signed the Kyoto Protocol. By November 2007, 175 nations had ratified it. (To be bound by the agreement, a nation must ratify it.) As of 2008, the United States has not ratified the protocol. It has refused to do so for two reasons. First, the U.S. government disagrees that developing countries should not be required to reduce their emissions. It argues that China and India are still classified as developing countries. But they are fast becoming industrial giants and major producers of green-

house gases. American leaders also worry that following the protocol will strain the U.S. economy.

So far, the results of the Kyoto Protocol have been mixed. Some developed countries, mostly in Europe, have managed to reduce their output of greenhouse gases. But overall, levels of these substances in the atmosphere are still rising. This is because some other nations now produce more of these gases than they did in the 1990s. In particular, emissions by the United States, by far the largest producer of greenhouse gases, rose by 16 percent between 1990 and 2004.

The obligations of the Kyoto agreement expire in 2012. Discussions at the U.N. about a new, more effective future protocol began in 2007. The 27 members of the European Union met in Paris, France, in March 2007. They agreed to cut greenhouse gas emissions by 20 percent by 2020.

Various smaller regional efforts to cut such emissions are also ongoing. One example is the Regional Greenhouse Gas Initiative (RGGI), begun

In April 2007, Thai protesters gathered outside the United Nations' Bangkok office to demand that world governments take action to revolutionize energy production.

in 2005. By 2007, 11 U.S. states along the East Coast had agreed to reduce their emissions by 10 percent by 2020. California has launched a separate program. It aims to reduce the state's motor vehicle emissions by 30 percent by 2016.

ENERGY ALTERNATIVES

One way that both nations and smaller groups are trying to meet these emissions goals is by promoting alternative energy sources. Everyone recognizes that the source of the problem is burning fossil fuels. Most of the excess carbon dioxide, for instance, comes from burning gasoline, oil, and coal. Turning to other, cleaner energy sources should lessen the emissions problem.

A large number of alternative energy sources are under consideration or already in use on a small scale. For example, cars and other vehicles can be powered by biofuels. These include various vegetable oils made from renewable crops, including corn. Although burning these oils does produce CO_2, the crops that produce them absorb an equal amount of this gas from the air. So no excess CO_2 is created in the process. Still, biofuels come with their own set of problems. The production of some biofuels can damage the environment by destroying habitats. It can

NOW YOU KNOW

One way to cut down on carbon emissions and slow global warming is to use public transportation instead of driving cars. The American Public Transportation Association estimates that public transportation saves 1.4 billion gallons (5.3 billion liters) of gas—or 14 million tons (12.7 million metric tons) of CO_2 annually.

also create other kinds of problems, such as food shortages.

Nuclear power plants produce energy on a much larger scale. Supporters of this approach point out that such plants produce very little air pollution and therefore do not contribute to global warming. Several nations, including the United States, already have a number of nuclear plants. Such plants presently supply most of France's energy needs. However, critics

HEADLINE
SCIENCE

say that these plants are extremely expensive to build and maintain. In addition, the nuclear wastes they produce are deadly and difficult to store. There is also the chance of some of the nuclear materials falling into the hands of terrorists.

Many people feel that energy from solar, wind, wave, and geothermal sources would be cleaner and safer. Solar cells change sunlight into electricity. Solar thermal panels can heat water or air inside buildings. Supporters point out that solar power has no

Solar panels capture energy from the sun and convert it into electricity; batteries can be used to store power for use at night or on a cloudy day.

fuel costs, is completely renewable, and produces no pollution or global warming. Wind power—electricity generated by large engines on "wind farms"—is also renewable and pollution-free. The same is true of geothermal power, which uses existing heat sources inside the planet.

EFFORTS BY FAMILIES AND INDIVIDUALS

As of 2008, these alternative energy sources exist only on a small scale. Most energy companies and producers are considering converting to them. But they say this process will be very expensive and slow.

Wind farms capture the energy of wind and convert it to electricity; as the wind moves across the blades of the windmills, causing them to spin, the motion is transferred to a generator, which creates electricity.

In the meantime, some families and individuals have started to do their part, however small, to fight global warming. The Natural Resources Defense Council and other environmental groups recommend steps that people can take:

- Write letters to elected officials and urge them to back environmentally friendly legislation.
- Drive energy-efficient cars. These are either electric cars or cars that get 40 miles or more per gallon (7 liters per 100 km).
- Replace standard lightbulbs with energy-efficient fluorescent ones.
- Weatherproof homes and apartments to reduce wasted heat and electricity.
- Turn off lights and appliances when not in use.
- Drive less. Instead, walk, bike, or ride the bus or subway. If you must drive, carpool.
- Eat food grown locally, which cuts down on energy used to transport the food.
- Eat less meat. The greenhouse gases generated by livestock make up 18 percent of the world's greenhouse gas emissions.

In these and other ways, people everywhere can help slow global warming so that future generations will inherit a healthy environment.

Compact fluorescent lightbulbs are four to six times more energy efficient than regular lightbulbs.

c. 1150–1460
First "little ice age" forces Vikings to leave Greenland

c. 1560–1850
Second "little ice age" brings abnormally cold
temperatures to portions of the Northern Hemisphere

1780
New York City's harbor completely freezes over

1912–2000
Eighty-two percent of the large glacier atop Africa's
Mount Kilimanjaro melts

1962–2001
More than 400 of the glaciers in the Himalayan
Mountains lose 20 percent of their volume

1970–2007
The percentage of the world's lands affected by
drought doubles

1973–2006
Carbon dioxide levels in Earth's atmosphere rise by
50 parts per million

1982–2007
The temperature of Earth's atmosphere rises by at
least half a degree

1986–2007
Major wildfires in the United States increase fourfold

1990–2004
U.S. greenhouse gas emissions increase by 16 percent

1995
A large section of the Larsen Ice Shelf in Antarctica
breaks up

1997
Most of the world's nations sign the Kyoto Protocol,
designed to reduce production of greenhouse gases

1999
Unusually warm, wet weather allows the West Nile
virus to enter the United States

2002
An even larger section of the Larsen Ice Shelf
disintegrates

2005
So far, the hottest year on record worldwide

2007
The United States experiences its largest number
of wildfires ever; European Union member countries
agree to cut greenhouse gas emissions by 20 percent
by 2020

2012
The original Kyoto Protocol is set to expire

Timeline

GLOSSARY

Atlantic conveyer belt
system contained within the North Atlantic Ocean that circulates warm and cold water, affecting the climate of the Northern Hemisphere

atmosphere
blanket of gases that surrounds a planet

carbon dioxide (CO_2)
gas in the air that animals give off and plants use to make food; greenhouse gas in air that traps heat from the sun

climate
conditions in the atmosphere in a particular place over long periods of time

climate change
global warming caused by human activity

drought
prolonged lack of rainfall in a given region

emissions
substances released into the air

feedback
process in which input and output within a given system form a loop and keep reinforcing each other

fossil fuels
fuels, including coal, oil, and natural gas, made from the remains of ancient organisms

glaciers
large masses of slowly moving ice

greenhouse effect
warming effect that happens when certain gases in Earth's atmosphere absorb heat and thereby make the air warmer

greenhouse gases
gases in a planet's atmosphere that trap heat energy from the sun

ice age
prolonged period of unusually cold weather in which glaciers and ice sheets expand

methane
colorless, flammable gas produced by decay of plant and animal matter

Northern Hemisphere
sum of Earth's land and water surfaces lying above the equator

ozone
form of oxygen that exists in Earth's atmosphere in small amounts and contributes in a small way to the greenhouse effect

precipitation
falling of water from the sky in the form of rain, sleet, hail, or snow

FURTHER RESOURCES

ON THE WEB

For more information on this topic, use FactHound.

1. Go to *www.facthound.com*
2. Type in this book ID: 0756535719
3. Click on the *Fetch It* button.

FactHound will find the best Web sites for you.

FURTHER READING

David, Laurie, and Cambria Gordon. *The Down-to-Earth Guide to Global Warming*. New York: Orchard Books, 2007.

Gore, Al. *An Inconvenient Truth: The Crisis of Global Warming*. New York: Viking, 2007.

Kowalski, Kathiann M. *Global Warming*. New York: Benchmark, 2004.

Minkel, Dan. *Global Warming*. San Diego: Greenhaven Press, 2006.

Parks, Peggy J. *Global Warming*. San Diego: Lucent, 2003.

Stille, Darlene R. *The Greenhouse Effect: Warming the Planet*. Minneapolis: Compass Point Books, 2007.

Silverstien, Alvin, et al. *Global Warming*. Brookfield, Conn.: Twenty-First Century, 2003.

LOOK FOR OTHER BOOKS IN THIS SERIES:

Cure Quest: The Science of Stem Cell Research

Goodbye, Gasoline: The Science of Fuel Cells

Great Shakes: The Science of Earthquakes

Nature Interrupted: The Science of Environmental Chain Reactions

Rise of the Thinking Machines: The Science of Robots

SOURCE NOTES

Chapter 1: Arthur Max. "Panel: Global Warming a Threat to Earth." *ABC News*. 6 April 2007. 12 Feb. 2008. http://abcnews.go.com/Technology/GlobalWarming/wireStory?id=3014590

Chapter 2: "Humans Cause Global Warming, U.S. Admits." *BBC News*. 3 June 2002. 12 Feb. 2008. http://news.bbc.co.uk/1/hi/world/americas/2023835.stm

Chapter 3: Bill Blakemore. "NASA: Danger Point Closer Than Thought From Warming." *ABC News*. 29 May 2007. 12 Feb. 2008. http://abcnews.go.com/Technology/story?id=3223473&page=1

Chapter 4: Patrick L. Barry. "A Chilling Possibility." *NASA*. 5 March 2004. 12 Feb. 2008. http://science.nasa.gov/headlines/y2004/05mar_arctic.htm

Chapter 5: John W. Anderson. "E.U. Raises Bar in Fight Against Global Warming." *The Washington Post*. 10 March 2007. 12 Feb. 2008. www.washingtonpost.com/wp-dyn/content/article/2007/03/09/AR2007030901992.html

ABOUT THE AUTHOR

In addition to his numerous acclaimed volumes on ancient civilizations, historian Don Nardo has published several studies of modern scientific discoveries and phenomena. He has also written biographies of scientists Charles Darwin and Tycho Brahe. Nardo lives with his wife, Christine, in Massachusetts.

INDEX